THE HOXNE T~~REA~~~~S~~

THE HOXNE TREASURE
AN ILLUSTRATED INTRODUCTION

ROGER BLAND
AND CATHERINE JOHNS

PUBLISHED FOR THE TRUSTEES OF THE BRITISH MUSEUM
BY BRITISH MUSEUM PRESS

ACKNOWLEDGEMENTS

This short publication is only an interim statement, but the work which made it possible nevertheless involved much effort by many people. The authors would like to thank the finder, Eric Lawes, the farmer of the land where the treasure was found, Peter Whatling, and the landowners, Suffolk County Council; Judith Plouviez, John Newman, and all those from the Suffolk Archaeological Unit who took part in the excavation; the coroner, George de Lacroix; and at the British Museum, Andrew Burnett, Michael Cowell, Su Dale, Stephen Dodd, Simon Dove, Frances Dunkels, Celestine Enderly, Joanne Freeman, Ray Gardner, Peter Guest, Andrew Hamilton, Richard Hobbs, Marilyn Hockey, Duncan Hook, John Hore, Chaz Howson, Janet Lang, Janet Larkin, Sandra Marshall, Vardit Melitz, Simon Muirhead, Sarah Newcombe, Andrew Oddy, Renée Pfister, Tim Potter, Jim Rossiter, Simon Tuttie, Julia Walton, Ray Waters, Dave Webb and Jonathan Williams.

©1993 The Trustees of the British Museum

Reprinted, with revisions, 1994

Published by British Museum Press
a division of British Museum Publications Ltd
46 Bloomsbury Street London WC1B 3QQ

British Library Cataloguing in Publication Data
A catalogue record for this book is available from the British Library

ISBN 0 7141 2301 3

Designed by Bernard Friedman
Printed in Great Britain by BAS Printers Limited Over Wallop Hampshire

HALF-TITLE
This stylized bust of a late-Roman Empress is hollow and was designe to be used as a pepper-pot. Details of the hair and clothing, and the imposing necklace arour the figure's neck, are embellished with gilding Cat. no. 33
Height 10.3 cm
FRONTISPIECE
General view of coins from the Hoxne hoard

CONTENTS

Reverse of a gold *solidus* of Arcadius from mint of Rome showing the seated figures of Rome (left) and Constantinople (right) with (above) the Christian Chi-Rho symbol. This coin, which is only the second known example with this design, typifies the division of the empire into its western and eastern halves, which became permanent after AD 395.

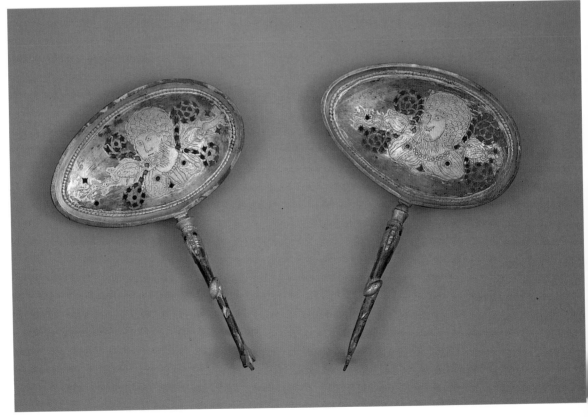

INTRODUCTION

The Hoxne hoard is one of the largest Roman treasures ever to have been discovered in Britain. It consists of some 14,865 coins and around 200 other gold and silver objects, and was buried by its original owners during the early fifth century AD.

The hoard was discovered in November 1992 and was brought to the British Museum for initial cleaning, conservation and cataloguing. On 3 September 1993, it was declared Treasure Trove (*see below*) at a Coroner's inquest in Lowestoft, and in November the Treasure Trove Reviewing Committee, after taking extensive advice, valued the whole find at £1,750,000. In April 1994 the British Museum succeeded in raising this sum, with the aid of generous donations from the National Heritage Memorial Fund, the National Art Collections Fund and others, and a substantial loan. The whole sum was paid to the finder, who has announced his intention of sharing it with Mr Whatling, the tenant farmer.

The work carried out in the Museum between the time of discovery and the Treasure Trove inquest involved curators in the Departments of Coins and Medals and Prehistoric and Romano-British Antiquities, expert archaeological conservators, scientists in the Museum's Research Laboratory and photographers. The aim was to complete the field excavation, to clean and stabilise the objects to ensure that their condition would not deteriorate, to classify and catalogue them and arrange them safely in custom-made storage trays, to carry out analyses of the metal compositions, to make a full photographic record of every piece, to prepare a report to present to the inquest, and to place the hoard on temporary exhibition immediately after the inquest to enable the public to view it. This essential basic work is only the beginning of the study of the treasure. The detailed scholarly research, as well as full

ABOVE LEFT Three bracelets in fine *opus interrasile* (pierced work). The design was punched and cut to produce a lacy pattern. The Hoxne bracelets are the first examples of their type to have been found in Britain.
Cat. nos. 27-29

LEFT The pair of transverse spoons from the gilded set represents a hitherto unknown type. There is also a pair of plainer spoons of this form in the treasure. The handles are in the form of dolphins, which also feature in the decoration of the bowl. The central figure may be a sea-god.
Cat. nos. 62, 63
Length of bowls 8.5 cm.

7

cleaning and restoration to exhibition standard, which can begin now
that the treasure has entered the national collection, will take many
years.

It is not certain who originally owned the hoard, though several
objects are inscribed with the name Aurelius Ursicinus, but it is likely
that it represents the accumulated wealth of a very affluent private
family. No trace of Roman occupation is known from the immediate
area where the treasure was found, though two miles away, at Scole,
there is a small Roman settlement on the Roman road from Colchester
to Caistor-by-Norwich.

TREASURE TROVE

Treasure Trove may be defined as objects of gold or silver which have been deliberately hidden with the intention of recovery, and of which the original owner cannot be traced. Any find which appears to qualify should be reported to the police and is subject to a Coroner's inquest. If the jury at the inquest decides that the find satisfies these conditions, it is declared Treasure Trove, and is the property of the Crown. It is then possible for the British Museum or another museum to acquire it on payment of a sum equal to its full market value as determined by an independent committee. That sum is passed on to the finder of the treasure by the Department of National Heritage as an *ex gratia* reward.

Each of this set of 10 spoons (five of each principal type) is engraved with the words AVRVRSICINI, 'of (i.e. belonging to) Aur[elius] Ursicinus'. Cat. nos. 81-90

LEFT Six of the Hoxne bracelets. The largest was intended to be worn on the upper arm.

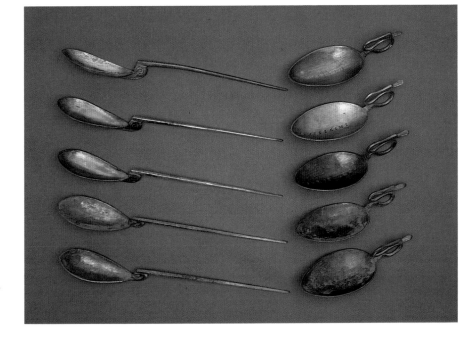

The five silver bowls.
Cat. nos. 37-41.
Diameter of shallow
dish (no. 41), 19.9 cm.

The silver bowls during
excavation in the
laboratory, showing the
organic material which
was used to separate and
pad them before burial.

DISCOVERY AND EXCAVATION

The Hoxne treasure was discovered by Eric Lawes on 16 November 1992 while he was searching with a metal-detector for a friend's lost hammer in a field at Hoxne, Suffolk. With commendable promptness, Mr Lawes reported the find on the same day and refrained from attempting to dig up the whole assemblage himself. On the next day, a team from the Suffolk Archaeological Unit under the direction of Judith Plouviez was able to mount an emergency excavation of the site, and all the objects had been recovered by nightfall on 17 November. They were collected and brought to the British Museum on the 18th.

The excavation team lifted much of the deposit in sections without separating compact groups of items. This allowed the detailed excavation and recording to be completed under ideal conditions in a conservation laboratory in the British Museum. Each of the sections had been given its own context number during the initial raising of the treasure, so that the relationship of elements within the deposit could eventually be re-created on paper and studied.

The excellent condition and completeness of the treasure is entirely due to the early involvement of professional archaeologists. The method of excavation has not only given us a rare insight into the way in which a major hoard was packed for concealment, but has also ensured the survival of items which would otherwise have been lost or inadvertently destroyed. For example, minute fragments of woven textile and decorative bone inlay have been preserved, as have tiny broken fragments of fragile silver sheet belonging to some of the more delicate objects. Some of the most interesting objects in the treasure, which can ultimately be restored almost to their original appearance, would no longer exist at all if the finder had not behaved so responsibly and invoked professional help.

3

EVIDENCE FOR
THE CONTAINERS

The professional excavation of the Hoxne treasure, both in the field and subsequently in the Museum, has enabled us to record details of the way in which it was buried. The extent of the deposit, which was clearly demarcated in the sandy soil, together with the presence of many rusted iron fittings, testify to a wooden chest measuring about 60 x 45 x 30 cm. None of the wood survived. The small silver locks and fittings described below (p. 28) obviously did not come from the robust box which contained the whole treasure but from smaller caskets within it. Also from a small box are the minute pieces of bone inlay decorated with circles and simple engraved lines which were found amongst the coins. There are over 150 such fragments, many of them tiny squares with sides 6-7 mm long. A few small fragments of an ornately carved cylindrical box (or *pyxis*) in bone or ivory were also found, and the small fragments of textile indicate that some groups of objects may have been wrapped in cloth.

Two small silver padlocks belonged to caskets deposited inside the wooden chest. Width 2.3 and 2 cm. Cat. nos 154, 155

All this evidence can be more fully studied and interpreted now that the treasure will be preserved in its entirety in a museum collection. Though far less beautiful and appealing than the precious-metal objects, the base-metal and organic fragments are of the highest importance if we wish to understand the circumstances in which the hoard was buried.

4

THE COINS

In all, some 14,865 coins have been recovered of which 569 are gold, 14,205 silver and 24 bronze. The gold coins are all of the denomination known as the *solidus*, weighing around 4.4 grams with a fineness of 99 per cent. All the gold coins post-date Valentinian ı's reform of AD 365-8, and indeed most of them were made during the reigns of Arcadius and Honorius, between AD 394 and about 405. However, eight different Roman emperors are represented in all. The gold coins are in an excellent state of preservation and, because none of them was more than about fifty years old at the time when the hoard is likely to have been buried, they have seen very little wear.

The base metal coins include twenty-four small bronze coins of the fourth century AD, but unfortunately most of them are so poorly preserved that precise identification is impossible.

The great bulk of the coins are made of silver and all have a purity of at least ninety per cent. Most notably, there are sixty light *miliarenses*, which weigh around 4.2 grams. All coins of this denomination are rare and the Hoxne specimens include as many as five unpublished varieties. The oldest coin in the hoard is a very worn *miliarensis* of Constantine ıı (AD 337-40). Most of the silver coins, however, are *siliquae*: apart from two coins made before this denomination was reduced in weight in AD 358, the remaining 14,205 specimens are all made on the reduced standard of around two grams. Finally there are also four half-*siliquae* of Arcadius and Honorius and one anonymous half-*siliqua*.

Fifteen different emperors are represented in all on the silver coins, and, apart from the one specimen of Constantine ıı, they were all minted within a period of fifty years, between AD 358 and 408. This conforms to the normal pattern of hoards of this kind from Britain. The coins in the hoard were made at thirteen different mints in all, from Trier in the west through to Antioch in the east. Most of the coins, however, come from Trier, Lyons and Arles in Germany and France, and Milan, Ravenna and Rome in Italy. There was no imperial mint in Britain at this time, except perhaps for a brief period in the reign of the usurper Magnus Maximus: unfortunately, the hoard did not contain any of his British issues.

The latest coins are two *siliquae* of the usurper Constantine III (AD 407-11) which may be dated to AD 407-8. We know, therefore, that the hoard was buried some time after AD 407, during the period when the Romans effectively abandoned control of Britain. However, it is difficult to be certain of the precise date when the hoard was likely to have been buried since no more coins entered Britain after the reign of Constantine III and numismatists still disagree as to how long the inhabitants of Britain continued to use coins after the end of Roman rule there. It is, however, unlikely to have been for more than about twenty to thirty years, giving us a probable date of burial for the hoard between AD 407 and about AD 450 at the latest.

Silver *siliquae* found in Britain are often clipped around the edges with sometimes as much as half of the coin being removed, and at least eighty per cent of the coins in the Hoxne hoard have been clipped in this way. It is not known exactly when clipping took place – it seems to be a phenomenon that is unique to Britain – but it is likely that it could only have occurred after the breakdown of Roman authority in Britain from the end of Constantine III's reign. It is difficult to understand why coins should have been clipped, since they could hardly have gone undetected, but one possible reason was to try to make the pool of coins in circulation go further at a time when no new issues were entering the province. Certainly forgeries of silver *siliquae* have been found in Britain and they could have been made from the metal obtained by clipping: a recent hoard of 870 *siliquae* from Whitwell, Leicestershire, contained forty-two such forgeries, some of which are made from the same dies as forgeries in the Hoxne hoard. Some 178 *siliquae* from Hoxne have at present been identified as contemporary forgeries, although when the detailed study of all the coins has been

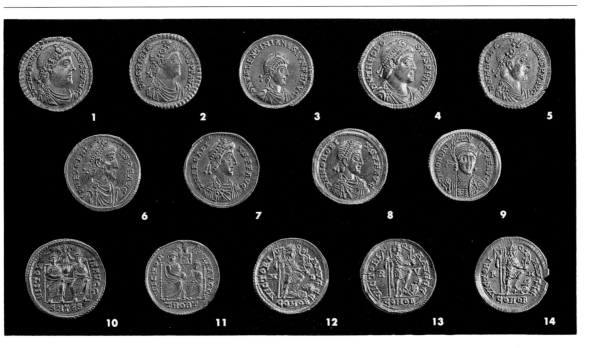

1-9. Gold *solidi* with portraits of Valentinian I (1), Gratian (2), Valentinian II (3), Theodosius I (4), Magnus Maximus (5), Eugenius (6), Arcadius (7) and Honorius (8-9). By this time imperial portraits had become idealised icons so that there are only subtle differences between the profile busts of these eight emperors (with the exception of Eugenius, who is shown bearded, perhaps indicating that he was a pagan). On the other hand, coins struck in the eastern part of the Empire after AD 395, such as (9), show the emperor's bust full-face. **10-11**. Reverses of *solidi* of AD 367-92 with the legend VICTORIA AVGG showing two emperors enthroned, being crowned by Victory and holding a globe. The pair on no. 10 represent Valentinian I and Valens, while no. 11 shows Gratian and the boy-emperor, Valentinian II, who is shown as the smaller of the two. **12-14**. Reverses of *solidi* of AD 393-405 with the legend VICTORIA AVGGG, showing an emperor trampling on a barbarian enemy, from the mints of Milan (12), Ravenna (13) and Rome (14).

completed the final number will certainly be very much higher.

The most remarkable feature of the coin element of the hoard therefore is its sheer size. Hoards of gold and silver Roman coins of this period are relatively common from Britain: more than eighty-five such deposits are known, but these finds are all much smaller than Hoxne and generally they contain no more than a few hundred coins. Thus the largest number of silver coins of this period found not just in Britain, but anywhere within the Roman empire was about 3,000 in a hoard found at Cleeve Prior in Worcestershire in 1811: this find was also said to have contained around 500 gold coins, but it was not properly recorded at the time. (It is a curious feature of coin circulation at this

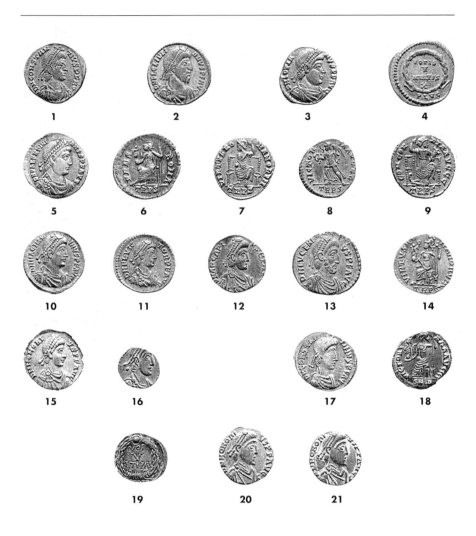

1-4. Silver *siliquae* of
Constantius II (1), Julian (2)
and Jovian (3) with revers[e]
referring to the vows (*Vot*[a]
taken by the emperors on
their accession and at
intervals during their reig[n]
(4). **5-6**. *Siliquae* of
Valentinian I (5) with the V[RBS]
ROMA ('the city of Rome')
reverse (6).
7-9. *Siliquae* of Gratian,
Valentinian II and
Theodosius I. Between AD [382]
and 383 these emperors e[ach]
had a different reverse typ[e].
Gratian had VIRTVS ROMAN[O]
with a figure of Roma sea[ted]
(7); Valentinian II had VICT[ORIA]
AVGGG with a figure of Vic[tory]
(8) and Theodosius I had
CONCORDIA AVGGG with a fig[ure]
of Constantinopolis seate[d]
(9). **10-11**. *Siliquae* of Magn[us]
Maximus and his son Flav[ius]
Victor. They continued usi[ng]
the VIRTVS ROMANORVM (7) a[nd]
CONCORDIA AVGGG (9) revers[es].
12-14. *Siliquae* of Arcadius
(12) and Eugenius (13). A
new reverse type with the
legend VIRTVS ROMANORVM
showing Roma seated left
(14) was introduced in AD
392. **15-16**. *Siliquae* of
Honorius. After AD 394 the
minting of gold and silver
coins was switched from
Trier to Milan and the last
major issues in the hoard
were made at Milan betw[een]
AD 393 and 402 (15). Most [of]
the *siliquae* in the hoard w[ere]
clipped around the edges [to]
greater or lesser extent, bu[t]
however heavily clipped [they]
are, the emperor's portra[it is]
left intact (16). **17-18**. Two
siliquae of Constantine III. [The]
latest coins in the hoard
are these two *siliquae* mint[ed]
at Lyons with the reverse

time that, with a very few exceptions, hoards of silver *miliarenses* and
siliquae are only found in two parts of the Roman empire: Britain and
Romania. This is particularly surprising since these coins were struck
at mints all over the empire, and hoards of gold coins of this period
have been discovered all over the empire.)

The largest hoard of Roman gold coins found in Britain whose contents can definitely be confirmed was the Corbridge, Northumberland
hoard of 160 gold *aurei* of the first and second centuries AD, although
there is a record of a hoard of 650 gold coins of emperors from
Valentinian I to Honorius and Constantine III (very similar to the Hoxne

1-5. Silver *miliarenses* with portraits of Constantine II (1), Constantius II (2), Valens (3), Arcadius (4) and Eugenius (5). These large silver coins contain some of the finest examples of imperial portraiture of the period. The coin of Constantine II (1) is the oldest coin in the hoard. **6-10**. Reverses of *miliarenses*. No. 6, of Constantius II, has a reverse design showing a banner with two captives which refers to the emperor's victories against the Persians in the AD 340s; no. 7 shows a figure of Victory inscribing a shield set on a column, while no. 8 shows the emperor holding a small figure of Victory and a banner, a type that was hitherto unknown for this denomination. After about AD 370 a new design was introduced at several mints including Milan (9) and Siscia (10) which shows the emperor holding an imperial banner and a shield. **11-12**. Full-weight silver *siliquae*. The hoard contained only two coins of this denomination and they are both of Constantius II; the first has a design showing Victory inscribing a shield held by a kneeling figure, while the second has been so severely clipped that only Constantius's portrait is visible. **13-16**. Half-*siliquae*. These coins were minted only occasionally at this time and the hoard contains just five examples. The coins of Arcadius (13) and Honorius (14) have a reverse design showing Victory (15); there was also a rare anonymous half-*siliqua* with a bust of Roma (16).

OPPOSITE CONTINUED
showing Victory seated to the left, dated to AD 407-8 (all the coins of Honorius, who did not die until 423, pre-date Constantine III's reign).
19-21. Forgeries of *siliquae*. The hoard contains hundreds of copies of *siliquae* with either illiterate inscriptions or crude designs.

solidi) found at the neighbouring village of Eye in about 1780. Unfortunately, as with the Cleeve Prior find, the coins from the Eye hoard cannot be identified today and the account that has come down to us is so vague that we cannot be sure whether there is any connection between the Eye and the Hoxne finds, although local records suggest that the find-spots were nearly four miles apart. Nevertheless, it remains a considerable coincidence that two finds containing over 500 *solidi* of the same period should have been made so close to each other and it seems at least possible that they might form two parts of the same deposit.

SUMMARY OF THE COINS

Gold *solidi*

Valentinian I (AD 364-75)	5
Gratian (AD 367-83)	12
Valentinian II (AD 375-92)	69
Theodosius I (AD 379-95)	20
Magnus Maximus (AD 383-88)	1
Eugenius (AD 392-94)	1
Arcadius (AD 383-408)	149
Honorius (AD 393-423)	312
Total	**569**

Silver *miliarenses*

Constantine II (AD 337-40)	1
Constantius II (AD 337-61)	2
Valentinian I (AD 364-75)	4
Valens (AD 364-78)	15
Gratian (AD 367-83)	13
Valentinian II (AD 375-92)	7
Theodosius I (AD 379-95)	7
Magnus Maximus (AD 383-88)	5
Eugenius (AD 392-94)	5
Arcadius (AD 383-408)	1
Total	**60**

Silver full-weight *siliquae*

Constantius II (AD 337-61)	2
Total	**2**

Silver reduced *siliquae*

(Note: the figures for the reduced *siliquae* are only provisional.)

Constantius II (AD 337-61)	320
Julian (AD 360-63)	892
Jovian (AD 363-64)	40
Valentinian I (AD 364-75)	217
Valens (AD 364-78)	1,420
Gratian (AD 367-83)	1,110
Valentinian II (AD 375-92)	575
Theodosius I (AD 379-95)	728
Magnus Maximus (AD 383-88)	1,034
Flavius Victor (AD 387-88)	156
Eugenius (AD 392-94)	525
Arcadius (AD 383-88)	2,265
Honorius (AD 393-423)	2,259
Constantine III (AD 407-11)	2
Uncertain	2,387
Irregular	178
Fragments	64
Unsorted	33
Total	**14,205**

Silver half-*siliquae*

Arcadius (AD 383-408)	3
Honorius (AD 393-423)	1
Anonymous	1
Total	**5**

Bronze

AE3 and AE4 of the 4th century AD 24

THE GOLD JEWELLERY

The matching pair of bracelets worked in repoussé with hunting scenes. The one on the right also includes a Nereid (a sea-nymph) with a mythological sea-beast which has the foreparts of a bear(?) and a fishy tail.
Cat. nos. 11-12.
Diameter *c*. 7 cm

Apart from the coins, the two principal classes of material in the Hoxne hoard consist of gold jewellery and small items of silver tableware such as spoons. There are twenty-nine pieces of jewellery in all, comprising six necklaces, three finger-rings, one elaborate chain ornament, and nineteen bracelets. All are of very fine workmanship, and, like most good-quality Roman jewellery, they are of very pure gold. The average gold content of the Hoxne jewellery is 94.7 per cent, significantly higher than the modern 22 carat standard, which is 91.6 per cent.

The finger-rings are of normal late-Roman types with filigree work and settings for coloured glass or semi-precious stones. These stones had been removed before burial. Gemstones with engraved devices were highly prized, and in the late-Roman period, when fine examples were increasingly difficult to obtain, they were often re-set several times in new gold mounts as jewellery fashions evolved. Two of the three rings were threaded onto one of the necklaces, while the third, a large and well-worn example with a rectangular bezel, was found during the laboratory excavation of one of the coin contexts.

Most of the necklace chains are made of fine loop-in-loop (foxtail)

chain which gives the appearance of a finely knitted cord or strap, and have decorative clasps; two have animal-head terminals where the chain joins the clasp, lion heads in one case and dolphins in the other, while another chain has a tiny Christian symbol, a monogram cross, worked in filigree on the fastener. All these chains would have been worn with separate pendants, but these were not buried with them.

The most elaborate and imposing chain is not a necklace but a kind of harness or body-chain consisting of four heavy straps of loop-in-loop chain which passed over the wearer's shoulders and under her arms, united on the chest and back by decorative brooch-like elements. One of these plaques is a gold coin (a *solidus*) of Gratian (AD 367-383) mounted in an elegantly patterned gold border, while the other contains settings for nine gems, a central cabochon amethyst, four garnets of elliptical form and four round cells which are now empty but which probably contained pearls. Pearls often decay during burial. This combination of mauve, blood-red and white gems would have pleased the taste for colourful jewellery which was typical of the late-Roman world.

The body-chain is a very rare piece of jewellery, and would have been of high value (it contains nearly 250 grams of gold). Many

OPPOSITE RIGHT The body-chain was worn with two chains passing over the shoulders and two under the arms, joining on the chest and the back with two ornamental gold plaques. One of these elements contains a gold coin of Gratian mounted in a decorative gold border, while the other is set with stones, an amethyst in the centre surrounded by four garnets and four empty settings which probably contained pearls.
Cat. no. 1
Length as arranged
c. 38 cm.

OPPOSITE LEFT This terracotta statuette of a woman is of Roman date and was made in Egypt. It shows how a body-chain was worn.

RIGHT This group shows the chains and finger-rings from the hoard. The body-chain is in the foreground.
Cat. nos. 1-10

OPPOSITE This photograph shows all nineteen gold bracelets in the hoard. The large example in the centre back is an armlet which would have been worn on the upper arm. Of the others, it is possible to pick out two sets of four in matching designs at the back left and right, and a matching pair in the left foreground.
Cat. nos. 11-29

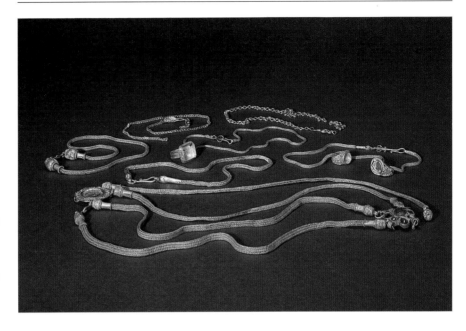

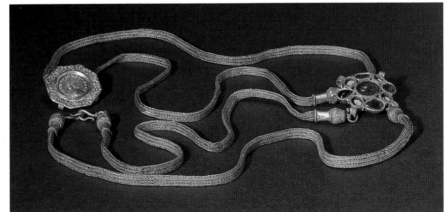

terracotta statuettes are known from Roman Egypt which show such items in use, but we cannot say if the chains were worn on some special occasion or by women of specific status. However, it is noteworthy that the Hoxne body-chain is quite small, and would have fitted an adolescent girl or a small and slender adult woman rather than a matronly lady.

The bracelets form a remarkable group, and the discovery of such a large associated group of gold bracelets is itself unprecedented. All are bangles, that is, rigid gold rings without any opening, which must be slipped on over the hand. There are two sets of four amongst them, one of which is of special interest because the style relates to a pair found in the Thetford hoard, a very similar assemblage of silver spoons and gold jewellery discovered in Norfolk in 1979. These are made of gold sheet in a ribbed and corrugated pattern which looks a little like basket-weave. Another matching pair is decorated with figures of animals and huntsmen in low relief. Several bracelets are made in the intricate goldsmith's technique often called *opus interrasile*, though this term may be a misnomer. It consists of extremely fine pierced work forming geometric or foliate patterns of lace-like complexity. This pierced patterning is found on some of the finest jewellery of the late-Roman and Byzantine world, but the Hoxne bracelets are the first examples of the fully developed style to be found in Britain. The largest

bracelet, an armlet intended to be worn on the upper arm, is in this delicate openwork technique. It has a diameter of about 10 cm, a width of 4 cm, and weighs nearly 140 grams.

The most important bracelet of all is in pierced work which incorporates an inscription in its design and must therefore have been made to special order by the goldsmith. The letter-forms and word-spacing are idiosyncratic, but the message can easily be read: VTERE FELIX DOMINA IVLIANE. 'Utere felix' (use [this] happily), is a motto often found on personal items and jewellery of this period, but here, in addition to the generalised good-luck wish, we learn that the owner was named Juliana, and was addressed as 'domina' (Lady).

The inscription of the Juliana bracelet 'unrolled' in a photograph taken with a special periphery camera.

OPPOSITE Four matching bracelets in grooved and corrugated sheet gold. Cat. nos. 13-16 Average diameter 6.5/7 cm.

The most remarkable piece of jewellery is the bracelet in pierced work which incorporates an inscription worked as part of the design. It wishes good luck to a lady named Juliana, the owner of the piece.
Cat. no. 29
Diameter 6.5/7 cm.

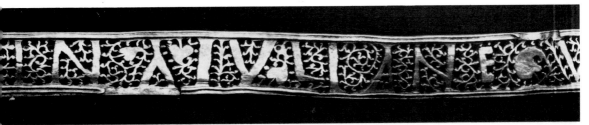

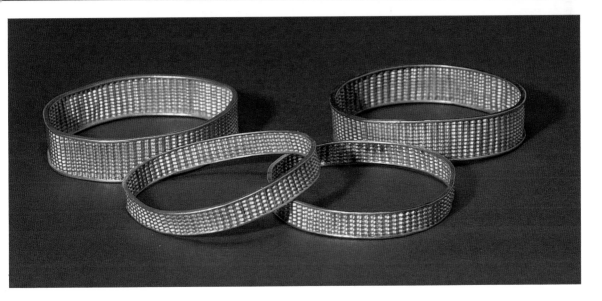

One of the finest of the silver objects is the solid-cast statuette of a prancing tigress whose stripes are inlaid in niello (black silver sulphide). The tigress is a handle from a large silver vase, and would originally have had a matching companion, perhaps a male tiger.
Cat. no. 30
Length 15.9 cm

The 20 round-bowled ladles form two sets of ten, one set with gilded abstract decoration on the handles, the other with an engraved scroll and the monogram cross within a circle.
Cat. nos. 42-61
Average length c. 14 cm.

THE SILVER OBJECTS

Silver plate, namely eating and drinking utensils made of silver, was owned by most wealthy Roman families, and could include large and highly decorated dishes, salvers, bowls and jugs as well as small containers, spoons and ladles. The Hoxne treasure was buried in a wooden box which was too small to contain vessels like the Great Dish from the Mildenhall Treasure, with its diameter of nearly 60 cm. Instead, the Hoxne tableware comprises seventy-eight spoons – nearly doubling the total number of late-Roman silver spoons known from Britain – twenty ladles and a variety of other small items including personal toilet implements such as toothpicks and ear-cleaners.

The most striking silver objects from the hoard look like statuettes, but all are in fact table utensils, or in one case, part of a larger vessel. The statuette of a prancing tigress with a long, elegantly curved tail and stripes inlaid in black niello was not designed as an independent object. It was one handle from a large vase with a slender neck and two zoomorphic handles. Two examples of such silver amphorae are known, one from the so-called Sevso treasure, the other from a hoard found in Romania (Conceşti). Though soldered joints generally give way during burial, so that handles are usually found separated from their parent vessels, the Hoxne tigress had been deliberately detached from her vase before burial; there was no trace of the rest of the object or of the other handle. The tigress handle may have been kept for its decorative appeal, but in any case its bullion value would have ensured its safekeeping with the family wealth: it is a solid silver casting and weighs nearly 480 grams.

The other four 'statuettes' are all *piperatoria*, pepper-pots. One is in the form of a bust of a late-Roman Empress depicted in a formal and hieratic pose, with details of the clothing, necklace and elaborate hairstyle picked out in gilding (see p.1). The Empress may perhaps be identified as Helena, the mother of Constantine the Great, who died in AD 330, but it is equally possible that this bust was not intended to represent a particular individual. Such busts are well-known in the form of bronze steelyard-weights of the fourth and fifth centuries, but the type is unknown in silver. The bust is a hollow container, and its separate base, originally soldered in position and standing on four small feet, has two heart-shaped apertures and an internal disc which can be rotated from the outside. It can be turned to reveal holes matching those in the base, enabling the bust to be filled with ground pepper, to close the vessel completely, or to align with groups of small perforations so that the pepper can be sprinkled. Pepper was an exotic spice from the east which first reached the Roman world in the first century AD.

The same mechanism is found in the other three pepper-pots. One is in the form of a solid-cast statuette of Hercules wrestling with the giant Antaeus. Its hollow base was the pepper-container. The other two pots represent animals, a reclining goat or ibex and a hound catching a hare. Both of these are very fragile sheet-silver constructions, and many broken fragments belonging to them were found in the careful laboratory sieving of sand from the context groups.

Two very small decorated silver vases have raised leafy designs similar to those on a silver jug from the Water Newton (Cambridgeshire) treasure, found in 1975. The other vessels in the hoard are five very plain little bowls, four of which were stacked upside-down on the fifth, a slightly larger shallow dish. These came into the Museum as a single context group (Context 0034), looking like a large lump of sandy soil. After the contents of the lump had been determined by X-ray examination, the bowls were carefully excavated in the laboratory. In the process, organic padding, probably hay, was found between them, and small traces of woven textile were recovered which demonstrate that the whole set was very carefully wrapped before burial.

Most of the other silver items are spoons or ladles. The latter have straight handles and deep round bowls. There are twenty of them, one

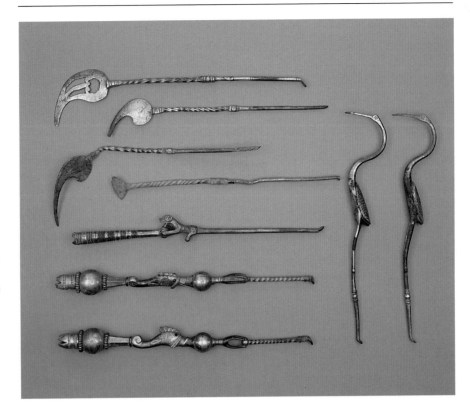

The nine toilet utensils from the hoard. The plain silver toothpicks with comma-shaped blades are a well-known type, but the ibis toothpicks and the dolphin and leopard objects are exceptional. The dolphins and leopard have a socket which may have held a cosmetic brush.
Cat. nos. 145-153.

matching set of ten with gilding and abstract decoration in relief, the other with simple engraved ornament incorporating the monogram cross, an early Christian device. The seventy-eight other spoons belong to two well-known late-Roman types and one completely unknown type, and they would seem to constitute the largest associated group of spoons yet known from any late-Roman hoard.

The known types are *cochlearia*, larger than a modern teaspoon with a long handle tapering to a point, and *ligulae* or *cigni*, tablespoon-sized with short curved or coiled handles terminating in the heads of swans or ducks. The new type is a perforated transverse spoon, a tablespoon with a pattern of holes and a short handle attached to one of the long sides. There are two pairs of these in the treasure.

The spoons include some matching sets, in particular one set of all three types with gilded decoration depicting dolphins and mythological sea-creatures, a traditional Classical theme. There are three small wine-strainers, familiar from many hoards of this period, and one much rarer combined strainer and funnel.

The remaining silver objects are nearly all toilet implements. They include combined toothpick/ear-cleaners of a common type as well as a pair of toothpicks in the form of long-legged birds, probably ibises, and three implements which include a deep socket, perhaps for a cosmetic brush.

Finally, there are two silver padlocks, a small silver hinge and a number of tiny silver angle-brackets and pins, and decorative rosettes in thin sheet silver: all these must have belonged to smaller caskets within the larger box, and constitute further evidence of the careful packing of the treasure.

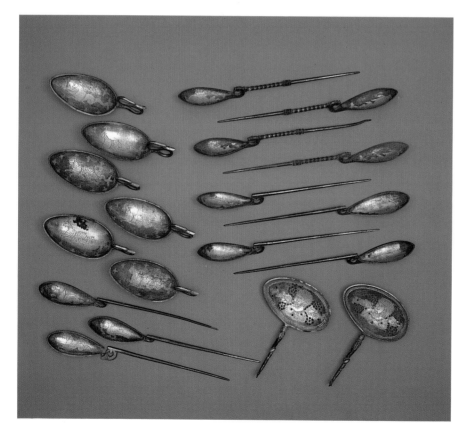

The matching set of 19 spoons with gilded figural decoration illustrates the three types present in the hoard. The long-handled *cochlearia* are about 20 cm. long.
Cat. nos. 62-80

THE INSCRIPTIONS

One of the spoons
inscribed with the name
of Aurelius Ursicinus.
Cat. no. 82
Length 11.3 cm.

Many of the objects in the Hoxne hoard have names and other inscriptions upon them. This is a common circumstance in late-Roman treasures of this type, but it is unusual to have such an extensive series of names and symbols.

Seven personal names appear on objects in the treasure, one of them, as we have already seen, on the bracelet belonging to Juliana. The name Aurelius Ursicinus is found no fewer than ten times, engraved and picked out in black niello on a matching set of ten spoons, five *ligulae* and five *cochlearia*. Several men named Ursicinus are known from historical sources, but it is not possible to say whether one of them is identical with the Ursicinus of the Hoxne treasure. Future research and perhaps future archaeological discoveries may cast further light on this question. In any event, the presence of a whole set of spoons belonging to this one named individual raises a strong possibility that the whole hoard may have belonged to him. Other names include Peregrinus, Faustinus and Silvicola, all on spoons.

Though many of the objects in the Hoxne find are closely paralleled in the Thetford treasure, which contains thirty-three spoons of the same late-Roman forms as those from Hoxne, there is one extremely interesting and important difference in the inscriptions. While the Thetford treasure produced a unique series of pagan religious dedications to the god Faunus, most of them combined with Celtic names indicating his worship in Britain, the Hoxne religious inscriptions are without exception Christian. Apart from the Chi-Rho monogram itself, the typical symbol of early Christianity, which is found on two of the spoons, two whole sets of tableware (spoons and ladles) and one necklace feature the monogram cross, a variant form of the Chi-Rho, and one spoon is engraved with the words VIVAS IN DEO (may you live in God), a common Christian phrase.

In demonstrating so clearly the Christian faith of its owner or owners, the Hoxne treasure is normal for the period when it was buried: it is the pagan Thetford assemblage which is exceptional. Nevertheless, the twenty-four Christian inscriptions form a significant addition to the ever-growing evidence for Christianity in late-Roman Britain.

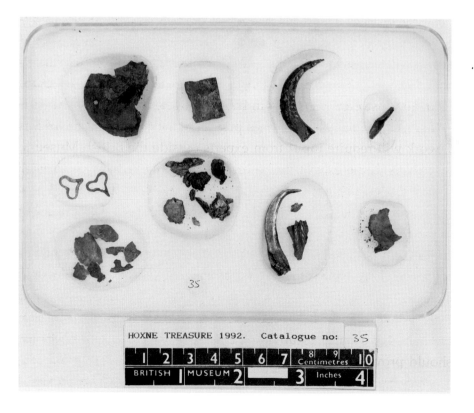

LEFT The additional fragments of the ibex pepper-pot in their storage box. They include part of the head, both horns and an ear, as well as fragments of the sprinkling mechanism in the base. Fragments of the object were found scattered in five different excavation contexts, probably through shifting of the contents of the box during the centuries of burial. Cat. no. 35

OPPOSITE The silver pepper-pot in the form of an ibex. Some conservation has been carried out to stabilise and support the fragile silver sheet, but many fragments are still detached.
Cat. no. 35
Height in present condition, 5 cm.

FUTURE WORK

The work which was carried out on the hoard in the nine months between its discovery and the Coroner's inquest has laid a sound foundation, but it represents only the first phase in a programme of scholarly research which is literally open-ended.

Now that the whole find has been acquired for the nation by the British Museum, the immediate priorities will be to prepare the material for display and to publish a catalogue which can be referred to by scholars working on Roman art and archaeology all over the world. The objects will be fully conserved and cleaned, and some will be carefully restored so that their original appearance can be appreciated (for example, the ibex pepper-pot will be reunited with the broken fragments of its horns, ears and head). New photography will be undertaken, and many of the objects will also be drawn for publication.

Comparable finds from elsewhere in the Roman Empire will be studied, and historical sources will have to be searched for possible further information on the names present in the treasure. Some of this work will require input from experts outside the British Museum. Analysis of the excavation records and photographs together with notes made during the laboratory phase of excavation should provide a detailed picture of the way in which all the objects were packed in the chest, and perhaps even the location and contents of the smaller caskets. Information of this kind is virtually unknown for major finds of treasure, which are usually dug up without any notes being made.

The identification, sorting and listing of nearly 15,000 coins has been a major task in itself, but there is much more research to be carried out on them. For example, studying the dies from which they were struck should provide evidence for the total numbers that were produced, while comparison with other hoards of the same period should throw light on the circulation of coins within the Roman Empire at this time.

Historical research is an ongoing and long-term process. Objects which have been in a museum collection for two hundred years can sometimes suddenly yield important new information because a new find relates to them, a new scientific technique has been developed and can be applied to them, or a new hypothesis has been published which changes our perceptions of them.

The Hoxne treasure has been exceptionally well excavated and recorded. The data present in the group as a whole is a precious archive which will continue to enrich and deepen knowledge and understanding of the late-Roman world for years to come, long after the initial popular excitement aroused by the discovery of treasure has died down. The acquisition of this hoard by the British Museum ensures that it will continue to provide enjoyment for the museum visitor and information for the scholar.

FURTHER READING

Brief illustrated accounts of the Hoxne find appeared in issues of the magazine *Minerva* throughout 1993. There are also short descriptions in the *Journal of Roman Archaeology* 6 (1993), pp. 493-6 and *Britannia* 25 (1994), pp. 165-73.

Roman Britain (London 1993), by T. W. Potter and Catherine Johns, gives useful background information for the general reader. The standard account of Roman Britain remains *Britannia* by S. S. Frere (3rd edition, London 1987); for this period see also *The Ending of Roman Britain* by A. S. Esmonde Cleary (London 1989).

The best introduction to Roman coinage is *Coinage in the Roman World* by Andrew Burnett (London 1987); for Roman coins found in Britain see *Roman Coinage in Britain* by P. J. Casey (Aylesbury 1980) and *Coinage in Roman Britain* by Richard Reece (London 1987). The question of late-Roman gold and silver coin hoards found in Britain is discussed by R. A. G. Carson in *The British Museum Yearbook* 1. *The Classical Tradition* (London 1976), pp. 67-82, while a list of such hoards is given by S. Archer in *The End of Roman Britain* edited by P. J. Casey (Oxford 1979).

On late-Roman silver and jewellery generally, the catalogue of the Thetford treasure is highly relevant: Catherine Johns and T. W. Potter, *The Thetford Treasure* (London 1983), while two booklets, *The Mildenhall Treasure* and *The Water Newton Early Christian Silver*, both by K. S. Painter (London 1977) are short catalogues of major late-Roman treasures from Britain. *Wealth of the Roman World; gold and silver AD 300-700*, edited by J. P. C. Kent and K. S. Painter (London 1977) is the catalogue of an exhibition of material similar to that in the Hoxne treasure.